GW01019204

HIDDEN TREASURES

LISBURN

Edited by Lynsey Hawkins

First published in Great Britain in 2002 by
YOUNG WRITERS
Remus House,
Coltsfoot Drive,
Peterborough, PE2 9JX
Telephone (01733) 890066

HB ISBN 0 75433 720 0
SB ISBN 0 75433 721 9

FOREWORD

This year, the Young Writers' Hidden Treasures competition proudly presents a showcase of the best poetic talent from over 72,000 up-and-coming writers nationwide.

Young Writers was established in 1991 and we are still successful, even in today's technologically-led world, in promoting and encouraging the reading and writing of poetry.

The thought, effort, imagination and hard work put into each poem impressed us all, and once again, the task of selecting poems was a difficult one, but nevertheless, an enjoyable experience.

We hope you are as pleased as we are with the final selection and that you and your family continue to be entertained with *Hidden Treasures Lisburn* for many years to come.

CONTENTS

The Poems

Seasons

Spring is my favourite time of year
Little lambs bleating in the fields I hear
Trees and plants, their little buds appear
Everything new and fresh, at this time of year.

I'm not so fond of autumn
It's windy, wet and dark.
I can't play outside
And I can't go to the park.

Summer is not too bad,
But I don't like the heat.
I spend my time at play
Instead of in school on my seat.

Winter brings the cold and snow
I enjoy the latter.
It's not so pleasant in the thaw
The drips go pitter-patter.

Andrew Stewart (10)
Carr Primary School

KILLER CARROTS

They arose from the earth,
Tall and thin, they had no mouths
Yet I could hear their ringing in my ears.
They had no eyes,
Yet I could feel their cold stare upon me.

In armies of 20, 40, 60,
They troop into town.
My family and friends screaming,
But the carrots storm on in,
No one can stop them.

All over the land,
All over the sea,
The whole world in their power,
Slaves kneeling on their roots.

Deborah Herron (11)
Carr Primary School

My Dog

Ellie my dog is black and white.
She is very friendly and does not bite.
She goes outside to play every day
And loves to chase the cats away.
When she comes in, her paws are all muddy
And I clean them because she is my buddy.
When night falls my dog dreams of her food,
But I love her because she is so good.

Jonny Orr (11)
Carr Primary School

THERE'S SOMETHING IN THE BASEMENT

There's something in the basement
Near the very, very back,
I can't yet see it
It's far too black.

It might be a *dragon*
With a sword from a knight,
Oh I really want to see it
I badly need a light.

What if there is also a *treasure chest*
With lots and lots of riches,
That he once stole off
Wealthy witches?

What if he's been living there
Quite a long while,
And the smell is dreadful,
Absolutely vile?

But

What if it turns out to be
An old, stray cat,
Living in the basement
In my old, woollen hat?

Debbie McKibbin (10)
Carr Primary School

A Rainy Day

It's raining now what can we do?
We can hear the rain dropping into the pool.
Drip, drop, drip, drop goes the rain
Splish, splosh, splish, splosh
All that mud is sticking to our shoes.
Mummy shouts 'Get out of my house
With that mud on your shoes!'

Robyn Dempsey (8)
Carr Primary School

JELLY

Jelly, oh how I love jelly
Jelly is my favourite treat.
Although it's chilly in my belly
I still like my jelly
'Cause jelly is my favourite treat.

David McGibbon (8)
Carr Primary School

APPLES

Apples, apples we all love apples
Apples sweet, apples sour
Apples are so rosy red
So sweet and so juicy too

Apples, apples, so red and green
Some sweet, some sour
Some fat, some small
Apples they're all the same!

Nigel Rea (9)
Carr Primary School

Kids

K ind
I mportant
D ifferent
S illy.

Andrew Mills (6)
Carr Primary School

Kids

K arate boys
I diots
D angerous
S illy.

Robert McGibbon (6)
Carr Primary School

Bananas, Bananas

Bananas for breakfast,
Bananas for lunch.
Bananas
Bananas
All in a bunch.

Some black and some yellow,
The outside looks yuck,
But the children who love them
They can't get enough.
Bananas
Bananas,
You're wonderful stuff.

You can dice them and slice them to lie,
You can spice them and make them into a pie,
You can dress them with chocolate,
You can press them with honey,
You can mix them with milk and make them all runny.
Bananas
Bananas,
You're lovely and yummy.

You can eat them with ice cream,
You can eat them and beam,
You can eat them with peaches,
You can eat them and dream,
Bananas
Bananas
You're as good as a scream.

Miriam McLaughlin (9)
Carr Primary School

Bare Tree

Long, snaking branches,
Naked, thick trunk,
Forked, fingered tips,
Undisturbed by junk.

No more birdies,
Nesting up there,
All have flown away,
Who knows where?

No more bunnies,
Bouncing round the tree,
All have hid away,
As swiftly as a bee.

No big, fresh leaves,
No budding flowers,
But never-ever ending,
The big tree towers.

Victoria Mayers (9)
Carr Primary School

COTTON WEEDS

I like words . . .
like fluffy . . .
just like cotton weeds . . .
in a field full of fluff . . .
just like a dream . . .
like a caster sugared bowl . . .
full of cream.

Adele Herron (9)
Carr Primary School

My Charmed Books

I like to sit down with a book,
It doesn't matter how they look,
As long as they involve something
That makes them very interesting.

My favourite books are called 'Charmed' books,
They are about witchcraft with lots of spooks.
Prue, Piper, Phoebe are so strong,
They have the powers to vanquish wrong.

My Charmed books are my best possession,
They're better than an English lesson!

Pamela Anderson (9)
Carr Primary School

Dogs

Dogs, dogs, I love dogs,
Fat or thin - St Bernard,
Tall or small - chihuahua,
Black or brown - spaniel.

I like them all!

Red setter, good with the gun,
My pet Ebony, full of fun,
I like to take her for a run.

Bailie, the Alsatian, guards me at night
And gives all the burglars a fright.

Christopher Anderson (9)
Carr Primary School

SAMMY

I have a dog called Sammy,
He is always in a mess!
He is either chucking food everywhere,
Or chewing my new dress!

He doesn't mean to do any harm
He's only having fun,
But what he thinks having fun is
Licking my scrummy bun!

Kristin Withers (9)
Carr Primary School

When I Went Outside

I went outside,
One summer's day.
I grabbed a doll,
And started to play.

In a hive,
Bees were making honey.
I got stung by one,
It wasn't funny.

Lyndsay Ebbage (10)
Carr Primary School

SAM

My brother has a dog called Sam,
He likes to bite my hand.
He jumps up on me when his paws are dirty
And slows me down when I'm in a hurry.

At night he sleeps in his bed
And barks in the morning until he's fed.
He thinks he's brave, but he's not,
Because he's afraid of our cat.
He also thinks he is cool,
But he really is a silly fool.

Katharine Tougher (10)
Carr Primary School

My Snow Poem

When the snow does fall
You hear the children call
The snow is like a little feather
It falls in cold weather.

You wear hats on your heads
You sleep in beds
If you slip on the ice
It would not be nice.

Katherine Macauley (7)
Carr Primary School

Whizz Kid

Becky's the best at reading
Samantha's good at sums,
Debbie's quick at counting
On her fingers and thumbs,

Anna's alright at writing,
Katy has lots of chums
But I'm the fastest out of school
When home time comes!

Samantha McFarlane (11)
Carr Primary School

A COLD WINTER'S NIGHT

There once was a chilly night
And there was hardly any light
There was snow on the ground
Which made a crunching sound
Whenever it was walked on.

There was a man out and about
And he saw firelight
He went to the window
And took a peep through
And saw a family eating hot stew.

He rapped on the door
And out popped a man
He said 'Hello my name is Sam'
Sam brought him in and let him eat
And let him rest his very sore feet.

Daniel Dunning (10)
Carr Primary School

Dogs

Dogs are fun,
see how they run,
they know their name,
some are long and
some are short,
when they are home
they like a bone!

Kyle Fullerton (10)
Carr Primary School

Snow

The snow is like a white moth.
It falls very slowly.
It falls like bits of Santa's beard.
It is very silent.
Sometimes the snow melts very fast.
The snow tastes like water.

The snow is like feathers.
It is like candyfloss.
It is like bits of paper.

It feels wet, wet.
It's very, very cold. It's like a blanket.
It's like ice cream.

Rachael Finlay (7)
Carr Primary School

Snow

The snow is small and cold.
It is soft and cold.
When I touch it, I feel numb.
It might taste cold and wet.

Jayne McGready (6)
Carr Primary School

Snowy Day

When I touch the snow it feels soft and cold.
Snow is so quiet I can't hear it.
Snow is like a white blanket on the ground.
When I touch the snow it melts in my hand.
When I walk in the snow it makes a crunch.
The snow is like feathers.

Susannah Foreman (7)
Carr Primary School

THE SNOW

The snow feels cold
It is like a snow fairy falling
Sometimes the snow is very cold
When I walk in the snow
I can make a crunch sound
The snow feels wet
I like the snow, I like it very much.

Sometimes I blow the snow
When I touch the snow it is very cold
It feels like Santa's beard
When I feel the snow it is soft.

It is soft, cold and wet
When I touch the snow it is cold.

Emma Stewart (6)
Carr Primary School

My Snow Poem

The snow is like a white blanket.
It falls like little bits of salt.
The snow feels cold.
It tastes like cold water.
The snow is slow, when it comes down.

Robert Johnston (6)
Carr Primary School

HIDDEN DEPTHS

Two friends went for a deep sea dive
Underwater they felt so alive
Thousands of bubbles floating high
Nearer and nearer, towards the sky
Floating seaweed, reefs of coral, shoals of fish
So many varieties make me wish
That I could share this moment with you
As it is such a fantastic view
The colours of the ocean bed
Will always remain in my head.

Rebecca Lister (8)
Harmony Hill Primary School

DOLPHINS

D olphins moving sweet and sway
O n its graceful way
L ovely and sweet
P laying joyfully and neat
H ollering sweetly, playing with other dolphins in the sea
I n the sea playing with me
N ow it's over sleeping in a sea cave
S o it begins with a twisting, turning and bursting wave.

Ashleigh Waring (9)
Harmony Hill Primary School

DOLPHIN KENNING

Water - jumping
Fins - swimming
Fish - catching
Body - twisting
Voice - squealing
Skin - shining
Crowd - cheering.

Callum Atkinson (8)
Harmony Hill Primary School

AUTUMN

Coming down from the trees
I see some crispy, brown leaves
Gliding, slowly, slowly, slowly
Landing with a tap on the ground.

Jack Boyd (8)
Harmony Hill Primary School

Under The Stairs

I like to pretend
The Hoover is
The snake

I like to pretend
My sister's doll
Is Dr Jones

I like to pretend
I am his partner

I like to pretend
The umbrellas
Are the torches
To scare the snakes

I like to pretend
The cupboard I'm in
Is a cave and I am on
The adventure of a
Lifetime.

Matthew Patterson (9)
Harmony Hill Primary School

VULCAN - GOD OF FIRE

People fleeing for their lives
    Terrified!
Fleeing from the sulphurous gas
    Choking!
Fleeing to safety
    Panicking!
Fleeing from the red-hot liquid
    Desperate!
Frightened children,
Weeping mothers,
Worried fathers,
Treacherous ruins,
    Vulcan's revenge!

Stewart Evans (8)
Harmony Hill Primary School

My Kitten

I'd like to have my own sweet kitten.
It would play with a ball of wool.
She'd also have my shoes all bitten.
But that's OK, because she's cool.
She eats her tea out of a tin.
But that's not right - she needs a dish.
The kitten finds things to eat in the bin.
Best of all she likes tuna fish.

Megan Porter (9)
Harmony Hill Primary School

DOG KENNING

Tongue - panting
Tail - wagging
Paw - begging
Heart - loving
Mouth - drooling
Sofa - stealing.

Courtney Speers (8)
Harmony Hill Primary School

A Stormy Day

Trees are swaying everywhere
Branches breaking here and there
Gates are flapping out their wings
The wind is blowing everything
Bin lids raising up and down
Clothes are blowing round and round.

Ashleigh Ussher (9)
Harmony Hill Primary School

A Stormy Day

I can hear the howling winds,
And the clattering dustbins.
These ferocious winds,
Are blowing people around,
And making tiny children,
Fall onto the ground.

The telephone poles that were once up straight,
Are now in a terribly bad state.
As the extremely strong winds,
Show no sign of abate.

These rushing winds,
Are making trees fall.
I can hear this powerful wind,
Making its call.

Colin Matthews (9)
Harmony Hill Primary School

A Stormy Day

Trees blowing side to side
Fierce winds
Storm force gales
Telephone poles falling down
It is a stormy day, a stormy day
Engineers out at night
Mending wires to put on the lights.

Michael Cochrane (8)
Harmony Hill Primary School

A Stormy Day

Thunder crashing and bashing,
It looks like the lightning is pounding the ground.
You'd think ten miles away
You could hear the sound.
The wind is pushing you back
The swaying branches are about to *crack!*

I wish I was in bed all cosy and warm,
Instead I'm out in this horrible *storm!*

Jonathan Patterson (9)
Harmony Hill Primary School

LITTLE TIMMY THE CAT

I had a little puddy tat
His name was little grey Timmy
He plays all day upon the mat
And teases his brother Jimmy

Some days he just wanders wide
Up the tall trees and down the glen
Into the wild green countryside,
But he'll always come home again

Once I thought he climbed up a tree
The Fire Brigade we tried to call,
But no, it was a catastrophe
It's not my cat but a squirrel small!

Stuart Black (9)
Harmony Hill Primary School

Under The Stairs

007 You Only Live Twice:

I like to pretend,
I'm 007,
The little old anoraks,
Are smart dinner jackets.

I like to pretend,
I'm 007,
The burglar alarm,
Is a nuclear panel.

And the old, dirty flannel
Is a mask of disguise.

My mission to complete,
Is to bravely compete,
With a man who is purely evil.

I like to pretend,
I shall defeat him with ease.

Rory McIvor (9)
Harmony Hill Primary School

UNDER THE STAIRS

I like to pretend
The shoes are the football boots
And the old towels are the shirts
I like to pretend
The hats are the crowds
And I am playing Man Utd
I like to pretend
I am the Liverpool captain
Scoring the ultimate goal.

Christopher James Moulden (9)
Harmony Hill Primary School

THE SWIMMING POOL

In the swimming pool you can see . . .
Water splashing
People dashing
Leaders explaining
Swimmers complaining
Babies clowning
Mummies frowning
People laughing
Daddies bathing.

Rachel Annett (9)
Harmony Hill Primary School

Under The Stairs

I like to pretend that:
The old papers are Egyptian scrolls.
I like to pretend that:
The rusty poles are huge pyramids.
I like to pretend that:
The crushed lids are pretty fans.
I like to pretend that:
The toy snake is the River Nile.
I like to pretend that:
The broken umbrella is the guardian of the tomb.
I like to pretend that:
The old string bag of marbles is my treasure of emeralds.
And I become Cleopatra and sit on my throne,
A battered cardboard box.

Rhiann Jeffrey (9)
Harmony Hill Primary School

A Stormy Day

One stormy day
I wakened to the sound of the wind
The trees rustling in the gardens
I peered through the curtains
There I saw the grass swaying

On the way to school
I saw the damage that the wind had done
A fallen tree lay on the ground
Its broken branches lay beside it

In the playground
As we ran around the wind pushed us along
Blowing shirts round our legs
Making our faces glow.

Emma Macdonald (8)
Harmony Hill Primary School

LINDSEY

L is for my auntie Lindsey whom I am named after,
I is for incubator which I lay in for a week,
N is for nature I love to see,
D is for decade I have lived only one,
S is for sister something I would like to have,
E is for eager to do well in school,
Y is for young - I'm the youngest in my family

Lindsey's my name - that's me!

Lindsey Freeman (10)
Harmony Hill Primary School

UNDER THE STAIRS . . .

I like to pretend
the mop is the witch's broom
and the trolley is the cauldron.
I like to pretend
the shoes are her boots
and the umbrella is her wand
and there are creepy cobwebs in corners.
I like to pretend
the pillow is her chair
and an old doll is her!
I like to pretend
she is sitting in her chair
and the tools are her specimens for spells.
Who knows what's on her mind!

Kathrine Humes (9)
Harmony Hill Primary School

THE KITCHEN

The kitchen is very useful,
In a most important way,
We cook all our food in it
Day after day.

The kitchen is full of interesting things,
You know when your food is ready,
Because the bell on the cooker
Rings with a ping.

We all get stuck in
And clear our plates,
Then slip outside and play with our mates,
Leaving Mum to clean the place!

Jenna Warnock (10)
Harmony Hill Primary School

SNOWDROPS

Snowdrops wriggle from the ground,
To see the sunray that they found,
'But where are our friends?'
Said one little snowdrop,
They were nowhere to be found.

'Mr Rabbit have you seen our friends?'
'No I have not, ask Mr Mouse.'
'There they are hiding amongst the leaves!'
'It's spring, it's spring' whispered the trees!

The snowdrops push up their delicate heads,
Through the dead leaves scattered all over the ground,
Their stems like green silk thread
Yes their beauty in the forest can be found.

Rachel Buchanan (9)
Harmony Hill Primary School

Mummy's Girl

Birthdays come, birthdays go
Always once a year
Sometimes Mum finds it sad,
And gives a little tear.
It means her baby is growing up
She is getting big and tall
I think that all the mummies
Would love us to stay small.

When we are small
They know that we are tucked up safe in bed
She reads us little stories
And kisses us on the head.
She looks at us and wonders
How her baby will turn out
Will it be quiet and shy
Or will it scream and shout?

She hopes we will be happy
No matter what life brings
And we will grow up
Safe and well
And have a life of wonderful things.

Amy White (10)
Harmony Hill Primary School

FOOTBALL CRAZY

Football is crazy and fun,
Good, to play with all my chums.
We play matches against other schools.
We do our best not to lose.

Mr Greer is our coach,
He always has the right approach.
Sometimes we can't play if it is wet,
All the boys in the team get upset.
We hope to win a cup for the shelf,
I would like to score by myself.

Matthew Briggs (9)
Harmony Hill Primary School

SPORT

Sport is fun and good to play,
I could play it every day,
Rugby, cricket, hockey, football,
There's a game for you, big or small.

Join a club; be in a team,
This is what I mean.
Hit, throw, kick, catch,
Either way you have a match.

A whistle goes, the game is on,
Players compete to the final gong,
Win or lose, it's all the same,
Taking part is the name of the game!

Stephen Hunter (10)
Harmony Hill Primary School

MY TREASURES

I have some treasures I want to show,
I have some treasure, you might like to know,
These treasures are my beloved pets,
My dad does not like them, he gives me threats.

My dog, Shadow, she's gentle and fat,
One of her hobbies is chasing our cat,
My cat is called Jess, she's black and white,
When she eyes up the hamster, she gives it a fright,
My hamster's called Scampie, she's fluffy and cute,
When she climbs her cage, she then slides down her chute.

Next, there're my goldfish, I won them at the fair,
They swim round and round, but don't go anywhere.
None of these pets are hard to look after,
When I see them play, they fill me with laughter.

Joe Murphy (9)
Harmony Hill Primary School

HIDDEN TREASURES

Most hidden treasures
You think can be found
In a ship long forgotten
Or buried underground,

But not all hidden treasure
Is made out of gold
It's not made out of silver
Or anything old,

My family's my treasure
It's my mum and dad
It's my little sister
For she's not that bad.

Abbey Tait (9)
Harmony Hill Primary School

A Stormy Day

It's a fierce, stormy day
And there're no ships at sea today,
The crashing waves, they rise so high
They almost reach up to the sky.
The howling wind rushes through the trees
Making a cold, windy breeze.

The wind blowing trees and toys
Still making its fierce, loud noise,
Outside on a freezing day
All trees moving with a sway.
You watch the storm from the windowpane
As the leaves drop down in the falling rain.

Christopher Nimmon (9)
Harmony Hill Primary School

A Stormy Day

Trees swishing, leaves rushing,
It's such a stormy day.
Thunder booming, lightning crashing,
It's such a stormy day.
The wind is tough
The wind is rough,
But whatever it's called
It's a stormy day.

Fionn Williams (9)
Harmony Hill Primary School

The Golden Gem

As I walked along the beach one day
I looked across and saw the bay.
I thought I would go and adventure there
Through the dark, damp caves, if I dare.

I went through the cave's narrow doorway,
And as I did, I left the bay.
My eyes got used to the darkened place
And my body got cold, as well as my face.

In the corner I saw something shine,
It sparkled and glittered at that time,
I ran over to the spot
As I touched it, it was hot.

A beautiful gem, within my hand,
I admired it as I stand.
It was my golden treasure
Giving me such great pleasure.

Lynley Megaw (8)
Harmony Hill Primary School

A Stormy Day

Today was a stormy day
Today the wind came out to play
It whistled round the corners
And howled down the streets
It crashed into the windows
And blew all the sheets.

Kimberley Hoppé (9)
Harmony Hill Primary School

TEACHERS

Teachers are pains
Teachers have a cane
Teachers make trouble
We make it double
Some children are bad
Teachers teach us to add
Teachers are cruel
We break the rules
Teachers lurk
Whilst we do our work.

Jessica Moulds (11)
Harmony Hill Primary School

A Giant's Pocket

An elephant for water
A chunk of land to eat
A car to play with
A person's shoe
An aeroplane as a toy
People to eat all up
A cow for meat
A list of things to get
Some human food to fatten the people.
Sellotape to stop the people from yelling!

Nicholas Gregory McKnight (9)
Harmony Hill Primary School

WEATHER

The weather is a mysterious thing,
You never know what it will bring.
Some days are wet, some are dry,
It all depends on the look of the sky.

I get confused with all of the seasons,
As the weather changes for all sorts of reasons.
Summer can be cool, autumn can be hot,
Spring can be warm - winter is not!

But whatever the weather, whatever the season,
And whether or not the trees keep their leaves on,
As long as we're healthy, strong and wise,
It doesn't matter what comes from the skies.

Mark Coughlan (12)
Harmony Hill Primary School

PLAYSTATIONS

P layful hours spent
L ocked in your room
A fter a time, dinner's ready
Y et why turn it off? You'll spoil the laugh
S everal hours have passed
T omb Raider, Driver 2, Star Wars Demolition
A fter three hours, you're still in your room
T iredness no longer exists.
I ncredible excitement
O nly ten minutes to bedtime, what a shame!
N ow it's all over
S o - *never underestimate the power of PlayStation!*

Stephen Coome (11)
Harmony Hill Primary School

A Hidden Treasure - Health

My health is very important to me,
I am glad I have my sight to see,
To keep good health, don't smoke or drink
And remember to wash your hands at the sink.
Keep fit by walking or playing sport,
Exercise helps get a good doctor's report.
Take medicine to help you when you're ill,
But ask you Mum before taking a pill.
Having good health is more precious than money,
Your future will be bright and sunny,
If you have your health.

Rebekah Hanna (9)
Harmony Hill Primary School

My Camera Never Lies

My camera never lies!
But 'Oh no!' my mum disagrees.
That can't be me with those big ears and wobbly knees.
My camera never lies!
'But that isn't me with those big red eyes,' my sister sighs.
My camera never lies!
'That can't be my chin all hairy and thin,' says my brother
With a cheeky grin.
My camera never lies!
'Surely that can't be my hair,' says Dad, with a stare.
My camera never lies!
Because it shows the truth, whatever your size!
My camera never lies!

Caroline Ferguson (9)
Harmony Hill Primary School

My Wish

My wish is to be a smart teacher
And I'd definitely not be a preacher!
I'd teach the children lots of sums
And award them all with jam-filled buns!
We'd go on many exciting trips
To see a tiger, lick its lips!
We'd have grapes and strawberries for our lunch,
How I love my happy bunch!
Sports day arrives, how they love to race,
I'll need lots of energy to keep up the pace!
My day at school ends quickly, or so it seems,
I wish them all very happy dreams.
Tomorrow is another day,
More lively minds, just what will they say?

Kathryn Dowse (10)
Harmony Hill Primary School

WHO IS HOLLY?

A waggy tail, deep brown eyes,
Soft coat, small wet nose,
Floppy ears, licky tongue
Sharp teeth which bite my toes.

Loving, friendly, cuddly puppy,
Snuggling in so close to me.
Looking up with sleepy eyes
Lying quietly on my knee.

Then she turns into a demon,
Starts to jump, to nip and chase.
Pouncing, boisterous, tumbling over,
Chewing on my good shoelace.
That's Holly!

Philip Rooney (9)
Harmony Hill Primary School

A Stormy Day

Black, grey storm clouds gather, quickly
Windows rattle noisily,
Wind whistling down the chimney.
Who's rattling at the letter box?
Rubbish blown round windswept streets
People huddle, harassed by the havoc,
Blustery rain turns menacingly
To rain, as sharp as pins and needles.
Schoolchildren battle across the playground
Coats held tightly, scarves blown wildly,
Wind pushing them quickly into school
Hair tossed untidily, hats lost happily.
Boats shelter, stormbound in the harbour
Wild, wonderful waves with foamy edges
Crash constantly on to cars at the seafront.
Turbulent tides toss ships, seasickeningly
New trees bending in the wind, nearly horizontal
Ancient trees creak, crashing to the ground,
Winds violently blow down buzzing wires
Snapping cables. *Lights out!*

Victoria Coome (9)
Harmony Hill Primary School

TREASURE TROVE

In a hidden cove
Was a treasure trove,
Opened gently, gold and silver did flow.
Where did the owners go?

When bloodthirsty Vikings took things
Of their liking!
Snatched from their owners
Radiant rubies
Shining silver
And dazzling diamonds.

Sparkling strings of jewels
Coins that simply glow.
All of this treasure
Plundered for pleasure.
So many years ago.

Marc Conlan (10)
Harmony Hill Primary School

My Pet Hamster

I have a pet hamster called Cookie
She likes her name
Now that's a shame.
I made a deal for a nice running wheel,
She sleeps all day and plays all night,
She makes a scratch and gives me a fright.
She loves to be cuddled and hates to be
Put in the bath.
At the age of five months, she climbed her cage,
She sniffs around and makes no sound.

Peter Kelly (11)
Harmony Hill Primary School

FOOTBALL CRAZY

It's the Saturday game again
The crowd has reached fever pitch,
The reds strike out a pass
Which turns out class!
As the keeper tries to save
The goal is down to Dave.
The blues kick back
They must not slack
It's time to score
Or they'll lose lots more!
The ball is in the net
It's a safe bet.
They'll be back to strike again
The coach is out to gain,
As they leave the pitch
It's over once again!

Chris Adams (10)
Harmony Hill Primary School

My Horrible Spell

In the cauldron you will go
My gran's smelly old toe!

A dead bat's wing
Let's add a bee's sting!

Hubble, bubble, let's make some trouble!

A lizard's eye and some poisonous pies
With some bad child's cries.

Hubble bubble, let's make some trouble!

Tail of a rat and an old man's
Pointed hat!

Hubble, bubble, let's make some *trouble!*

Danyelle Broom (10)
Harmony Hill Primary School

KYLE MARTIN

P eter's my friend, the very best
E ntertaining he is, with electrifying zest
T ogether we are the ultimate team
E njoying Pokémon, we don't run out of steam
R unning and tig to be first, is our quest.

K ing of the skateboard, he is a cool dude
E very day he practises his tricks, boy he's good!
L ike me, he loves PlayStation
L ego technic, we'll make a creation
Y ears together, our friendship has withstood.

Kyle William Martin (11)
Harmony Hill Primary School

HAPPINESS

Happiness is pink
It tastes of strawberry sundaes
And smells like a rose.
It looks like people smiling happily
And sounds like children laughing.
Happiness feels great.

Rachel Benson (11)
Harmony Hill Primary School

A Stormy Day

The winds blow hard
They whistle and cry,
The branches and leaves they fly.
The slates rattle
And the gutters fall,
Oh the wind must be having a ball.

Beth Long (9)
Harmony Hill Primary School

A Snowy Day

Flakes of snow fell on the treetops
Making them, oh so white
The soft white snow lies on the ground
Glistening in the winter sun.

Gordon Ringland
Harmony Hill Primary School

An Explorer's Pocket

Inside an explorer's pocket, you will find . . .

A map to help him find the way
A torch to see the way in the dark,
Boxes of matches to light some fires
A compass to show the direction,
Dollars he found in America.
Fossils from digging in the sand,
A rope, to help climb steep cliffs.
Bottles of water to drink when thirsty
Food left over from a meal.
A camera to take some photographs,
Photographs from lots of different places.

Stephanie Smyth (11)
Harmony Hill Primary School

My Attic

There is glass fibre all over everywhere,
It smells all dusty and gloomy,
People are rushing around outside in cars,
I feel all sneezy, like I'm in the Hoover bag.

There are no proper walls up here,
There are only bricks and a sort of material
That is actually the thing under the tiles of our roof
The wind is howling and rustling like an angry wolf.

It is scary up here,
It reminds me of a dream I once had.

The attic is brimming with cardboard boxes
The roof is held up with lots of wooden beams,
I am cold and can't wait to go back down the ladder
This is not my favourite place in the house.

Claire Stowell (9)
Harmony Hill Primary School

My Kitchen

TV blazing against the wall
Slight rumble of the PlayStation
A1 singing loudly
Rachel dancing like a spinning top.

The fresh smell of French bread and tangy orange juice
Grapes, as green as grass
Round, juicy oranges in a glass bowl
The smell of tea, bubbling on the cooker
Pencils scribbling softly
A toy dog woofing loudly.

My tummy rumbles
The doorbell rings
Dad says 'Get your homework done!'
The feel of a warm chair
The soft, gentle purring of my rabbit
Shiny cream blinds
Gleaming white walls
Wooden cabinets with glass shelves
I feel warm and relaxed
Calm and collected
In my kitchen.

Mark Campbell (8)
Harmony Hill Primary School

The Attic

Bags packed with old clothes
Creaking floorboards,
Fusty smell of old insulation
Cold and draughty.
Last year's Christmas tree, lying on its side
Boxes cluttered full of ragged books,
Water hissing through the pipes
Insulation like prickly cotton wool.
Damp and quiet,
The steady drip, drip of the tank.
Cobwebs hanging from the wooden beams
Noises from outside seem so far away,
I feel safe and relaxed,
But very, very lonely,
Up here in my attic.

Stuart Morgan (9)
Harmony Hill Primary School

A FREEZING MONDAY MORNING

I see the rain running down the shiny window
The still sky and grey clouds,
The dark classroom with bright colours on the wall,
The trees rocking and swaying from side to side.
Cars, vans and lorries going up and down the street,
The cold, cold trees, gaunt and bare,
Tall, proud evergreens
Wet, wet, soaking grass.
I can hear nothing
Nothing . . . nothing but the wind!
The cold, cold wind and the
Rain dripping from the foggy skies.
I feel cold.
Cold as if I have just come out of the sea
And on to dry land.
My fingers and toes feel numb on
A freezing Monday morning!

Sharon Kilpatrick (9)
Harmony Hill Primary School

A January Morning

Dripping branches
Trees swaying back and forth
Gaunt trees
Raining, like Heaven's crying
Roaring, whistling wind
Chilly air
Lorries from far distances
Saturated ground
Silent birds searching for wriggly, squirmy worms
Muddy roads
Tall, proud evergreens
Shallow puddles
Rain dropping into puddles like water from a tap
Numb fingers
Stiff legs
Wet windowpanes
And then a rough breeze brushing past my cheek.

Adele Rodgers (9)
Harmony Hill Primary School

My Living Room

Pictures of my brother and me hanging on the wall
Scented candles burning all around the room.
The brown clock going tick-tock, tick-tock
Two small dogs sitting on the wide hearth
A bright light shining like the sun.
Everyone talking around me.
The cold floor as I take my shoes off
Bunches of fresh flowers sitting on the wooden table.
I feel safe, comfortable in my own living room.
The delicious smell of cooking as my dad opens the door.
My sleek cat sitting on the mat
The soft feel of a velvet cushion.
Cosy and warm, when the heating is on.

Natalie Partridge (9)
Harmony Hill Primary School

HAPPINESS IS . . .

Ian Van Dahl on the radio
The crowd cheering when Liverpool scores a goal
Rubbing my dog's spotty tummy
Helping make the dinner
Eating my dad's spicy, hot chilli
Smelling sweet chocolate, melting on the hot cooker
Playing with Hailo, Mark's rabbit
Listening to my teacher's fab stories about
Mysterious ancient Egypt
Looking at the colourful posters on the classroom wall
The sound of the bell ringing in my back garden.
Linkin Park singing 'In The End'
The feel of my cosy, warm, fluffy blanket
The fabulous music at the start of the Cramp Twins
Playing with my dogs and friends
The soft feel of my cute Dalmatian teddy
Who sits on my bed
The sweet scent of my nanny's roses
Doing brilliant art in school
Eating warm, runny custard
Listening to Mozart
Playing 'Who Wants To Be A Millionaire' against my dad
Listening to my teacher read Jeremy James.

Tessa Young (9)
Harmony Hill Primary School

A Rainy Day

Numb fingers,
Cold ears,
Red cheeks
And little tears.

Whistling wind
Whirling by,
Dirty grey clouds
In the sky.

Green swaying trees,
Wet, damp roads,
Soggy green grass
And a red runny nose.

Cold, chilly air
And a wet, slippery ground,
Pitter-patter, raindrops
Splashing all around.

Zoe Bailey-Wood (9)
Harmony Hill Primary School

My Mum

My mum is better than the rest
She's kind and caring, she's the best.
Mum tucks me in at night,
She cuddles and squeezes me tight.
Mum makes me giggle and laugh
And always takes me to the swimming baths.
No one is more special than my mum,
She even lets me have chewing gum!
Mum is my hidden treasure,
She gives me lots of pleasure.
I love her kind and gentle touch,
I love my mum so much.

Becky Williams (10)
Harmony Hill Primary School

THERE IS A REPAIR NEEDED HERE

My dad's car is very old,
'It's a little gem' or so I'm told.
The door will not open!
The engine goes bang!
The seat falls back!
The clutch goes clang!
Out puffs the black smoke,
There is a repair needed here,
Would you believe it?
My dad's a car engineer!

Charlotte Irvine (11)
Harmony Hill Primary School

Our Hot Water Tank

Our hot water tank went piff, paff, poof
Oh dear, the water came through the roof
'Phone the plumber quick, quick, quick!'
The plumber said '£96 please!'
My poor dad, he fell to his knees!

Robyn Cairns (10)
Harmony Hill Primary School

How Other People See Me

To my parents I'm untidy
To my nanny, I'm helpful
To my neighbours, I'm kind
To my friends, I'm fun
To my teacher, I'm a chatterbox
But to myself, I'm just *me!*

Jamie McFarland (11)
Harmony Hill Primary School

My Dogs

My dogs are fluffy, shiny, silky, cute and cuddly white
Their eyes are sweet and adorable their personalities are bright
When they go for walks they come back, muddy and poor
But Tina is quite clever, my dog can open our back door!

When it comes to Molly, all she wants is attention
But Tina is active, she's a dog on a mission!
When they know what they want, they'll be determined and get it
Even if it does end up giving them a headache.

Molly is a groovy dog, with her shades on she looks cool
But the bad thing about them is, they always, always drool.
I love my dogs even if they always need attention
But what they need is just love and affection.

Debbie Cupples (11)
Harmony Hill Primary School

My Dog

My dog Boris
He is funny and
fluffy too. He
is the best dog
in the world.

He lays on his
back kicking his
legs in the air.
He bounces around
like a bouncy ball.

He is naughty
sometimes, but
inside he doesn't
mean to be naughty.
He loves his food
just like my dad.

Jenny Smith (11)
Harmony Hill Primary School

Rain

Rain is wet,
cold and damp
makes you shiver
like a jelly.

Rain is fun to play in
especially puddles
you run right up
and jump right in.

Rain is boring
especially when you're
stuck inside with
nothing to do.

Christopher Gill (11)
Harmony Hill Primary School

My Toaster

Our toaster was just doing fine
until one day at half-past nine
Bang! Puff, puff! Bang! Puff, puff!
Boom!
All of a sudden, smoke-filled the room
it lifted up into the air,
gave us all an awful scare.
Mother shouted 'Get your father. Quick!
That fright has made me feel quite sick!'

Jonathan Allen (11)
Harmony Hill Primary School

My Car

My car was so good
It could go really far
Its wheels were of rubber
It had masses of power.

One day it would not start
We thought it was broke
We rang the garage
Out came a repair bloke!

He said there was no sound,
No hum and no grind
It was the battery,
It was flat and not very round.

He put on some leads
And added a part
It jerked and it banged
Hooray it jumped to a start!

Chad Houston (11)
Harmony Hill Primary School

Broken Down

Our quad broke down
It went crank, crank!
Then crack, crack!
Oops! I broke the kick-start,
Quick! Quick! Repair it.

David Simpson (10)
Harmony Hill Primary School

HALLOWE'EN FIREWORKS

Red, green, blue and yellow too,
These are the colours of fireworks,
But only a few . . .
I like fireworks, how about you?

Shooting up into the dark
Then exploding with lots of sparks.
Light another, watch it go
Hear the people ooh and oh!

You may think that lighting them is cool,
But it can be dangerous
So ask an adult to do it
Please, don't be a fool!

I've got a few more things to say
Watch out for monsters that will give you a fright
And have a nice fireworks display
On *Hallowe'en* night!

Gavin Turtle (10)
St Aloysius Primary School

FIREWORKS

The Roman candle
The Catherine wheel
The magical fountain
Fiery rocket.

The raging whistle
The tumultuous roar
The screaming bang
On Hallowe'en night.

The spinning scream
Of the Catherine wheel
The blasts and bangs
Of the oncoming rocket.

Oh how I love Hallowe'en
So noisy, so bright, so beautiful
Oh how I love Hallowe'en
When demons rule the night.

Colm Tracey (10)
St Aloysius Primary School

JACK FROST

Jack Frost, Jack Frost, out to play,
Nipping my fingers and toes every day,
In the mornings I'm freezing cold,
Because of that horrible Jack Frost!

'Mum, something's killing me with frostbite!' I cry.
'He's nipping my fingers and toes.'
Jack Frost will get you no matter where you go.

Marie Fegan (8)
St Aloysius Primary School

JACK FROST'S SWORD

Jack Frost comes at night
He makes everything ice-cold and white.

When you go out he will nip you and you're like a snowman.
He spreads snow across the town.

Jack Frost comes out of his icy palace but on his throne he has to have
A sword made of ice to turn everything white.

Lee Nelson (9)
St Aloysius Primary School

Jack Frost

Someone's creeping through the night
And he's such a terrible sight
He freezes all he passes by
Like flowers that wither and die.

He sets on the ground his hand
And ice spreads across the land
Just before sunrise it's time to go
Then when you wake you find ice and snow.

In the daytime he disappears
And the frost that he leaves nips at your ears
When he gets home he starts to write
The plans for the next night.

Jamie Dennison (9)
St Aloysius Primary School

Jack Frost

He comes out of the Ice Palace in the cold winter's night,
He spreads across the town with his cold, nipping bite.
A blanket of frost flies over town,
The temperatures drop and the wind is biting.
I've warned you once, I won't warn you again,
Jack Frost is back to nip and cause pain.
He goes back through the clouds and disappears back to the Ice Palace,
Where he lies and waits to come again.

Hayley McKay (8)
St Aloysius Primary School

ICE PALACE

Jack Frost sitting on his icy throne,
Jack Frost ready to break all your bones,
Ice palace, so cold, so dark, so misty, not bright,
In the middle of the mountains,
His icy men going to work,
Ready to make it go cold,
Temperatures drop,
Frost goes, doesn't stop,
Making you nip in the night!

Daniel Mallon (8)
St Aloysius Primary School

My Kind Of Winter

In the bleak midwinter,
Snow on snow,
Foggy winds blowing deeply in the still ghostly air,
Puddles turn to ice,
Paths and roads covered in snow and fog,
And icy things everywhere,
So silent, so peaceful,
So cold yet warm,
Warm in my heart because I like it like this,
I really do, not noisy but quiet like me,
I still do not know why, but I like this much better,
So my kind of winter has finally come,
So silent, so peaceful like me,
This is the way I think winter should be.

Megan Rose McNamee (8)
St Aloysius Primary School

THE TELEVISION

There it sits in the room all alone
Waiting patiently for the kids to come home
Then suddenly he is glared at, observed
And watched throughout the day.

He hopes the children will go off to play
For he gets tired at the end of the afternoon
Eventually his button is hit off
So silently he falls asleep, *zzzzz*
Quietly and all alone.

Sarah Marley (11)
St Aloysius Primary School

HALLOWE’EN

Hallowe’en is coming,
It’s coming after you.
You’d better beware
It’ll come for you.
Oh please, please I’m really scared,
Well don’t be, it’s just Hallowe’en.
But it can control you, own you.
Chase you, so you had better be ready.
Oh look, it’s already here, watch out.

Rachel Agnew (11)
St Aloysius Primary School

SUMMERTIME

Summertime sun burns very hot,
You relax and it's like being cooked in a pot,
Then the ice cream man comes round,
Pours the cold ice creams all around.
Sometimes people make BBQs
And the fire roars, burning the food.
Then at night the moon is shining,
In the morning the sun is rising.

Stephanie Porter (10)
St Aloysius Primary School

JACK FROST

Jack Frost is coming to
Spread across town.
Jack Frost is coming
When the temperature's down.
We're numb with cold.
Jack Frost is bold.
He's nipping across
He's being the boss.

Laoise Earle (9)
St Aloysius Primary School

FOOTBALL CRAZY

Football, football is a brilliant sport,
Football, football gives you lots of fitness support.
Football, football keeps you well and fit,
Football, football, I've got the Man Utd kit!
Football, football, who's going to win the league?
Not Liverpool, of course, Man United have taken the lead!

Jack Walsh (9)
St Aloysius Primary School

I AM JACK FROST

I am Jack Frost.
These humans, huh!
They pollute the air with . . .
You know what . . .
Warmth!

They're crazy, warm is so strange
Why not be cold, it's fantastic,
They wake up to see a frost-smashed window,
They think they have been robbed -
They have!
It was actually me, trying to steal their warmth!

I never succeed.

Why oh why is there warmth?

Ciaran O'Meallaigh (9)
St Aloysius Primary School

My Cat

My pet is a cat,
He is all different colours,
He shines from his head to his paws.
He sleeps in his basket and snuggles in so tight,
Awaiting the sunny morning.
He wakes up to see me getting his breakfast,
Springs up from his basket,
He lets out a big 'Miaow'
He sits near his bowl and starts to eat,
Wondering today, what flavour of meat?
He is my pet and I love him to the end of his cuddly nose.

Claire Magennis (8)
St Aloysius Primary School

WINTER, WINTER, WINTER

Cold fingers, cold toes,
Rosy cheeks, freezing nose.
The only time I come out to play,
Is when the winter sun shines its rays.

Temperatures drop, Jack Frost loves that,
Hey, you cheeky little chap!

Glistening like a diamond,
Glittering like thin ice,
Glitzy like a breeze,
Rolling like a dice.
Making the land freeze.

Anthony Douglas (9)
St Aloysius Primary School

The Trees

Trees are standing way up high,
With rustling sounds of the leaves.

Suddenly a roar of thunder,
With a flash of a scream. *Aaah!*

Finally the storm rests,
Also the rustling sound of the leaves

Are all now very quiet on this autumn day!

Sarah McCaighy (10)
St Aloysius Primary School

Water

When water's angry, it stings and burns me,
It bites at my skin like a wild creature.
But then the water calms down,
And cools my burns and bites.
Water cools you down,
Deliberately helping you,
When water gently soothes your throat
And gives you strength it is *calm!*
Then water lashes out at you,
Hitting you, hurting you,
Now water is hot and angry.

Sarah Brookes (11)
St Aloysius Primary School

FROST!

Frost appears to be cold, wet and bright,
Frost appears mostly in the night,
It sits prettily on comforting flowers,
Then it runs away when the sun comes out,
I wonder where it went to?

Then night comes and *look!*
Here Frost comes running tiredly back to his comfortable flower.

Louise McMullan (11)
St Aloysius Primary School

FLAMES

The raging flames screaming and shouting
Chewing up paper and spitting out ash
The flames raging higher and higher
Burning the sky
Sucking the life out of leaves and branches
The flames are still enraged
Finally settling down for a rest
Then soon after pass away
To a pile of black ashes
Dead on the ground.

Leigh Graham (10)
St Aloysius Primary School

A Lesson To Be Learned

This is the story about my neighbour, Mr Brown,
When you read it a lesson will be found,
Because Mr Brown was not healthy,
And not to mention very wealthy,
He went to the doctor's when he was a bit of a mess,
The doctor said, 'Mr Brown you are a wreck, you're
suffering from stress!
To be very healthy you have to eat,
Loads of fruit and veg and cut down on meat,
Plenty of sleep will reduce bags,
Try cutting down on booze and fags,
And please try to exercise daily,
I'm sure you'll find it helps . . . *really!*
Mr Brown you are a disgrace
You'll never be able to enter a race.'
So poor Mr Brown took the doctor's advice,
He soon became healthy eating pasta and rice!

Michaela McMenamin (11)
St Aloysius Primary School

Titanic Goes Down

I saw a ship go sailing by,
So big that it could reach the sky,
The ship they said would never sink.
They forgot about icebergs, I think.
The grandest ship that set to sea,
All aboard the deck was me.
If I had a dream come true
I'd sail aboard Titanic, wouldn't you?
An iceberg hit the starboard side,
It broke in the middle and many people died.
I'll never forget that dreadful night,
When the Titanic was nowhere in sight.

Shannon Savage (10)
St Aloysius Primary School

The Sinking Of The Titanic

In a lifeboat I am sitting,
Full of shock as I watch the Titanic sinking.
I am cold and amazed, full of guilt
As I watch people in the water less lucky than I.
I hear people screaming, as I think, as they die.
Hopeless, I wait in this boat of doom.
Full of shame and shock.
The ocean has their lives.
Then I see the Titanic has gone.

It's sinking.

Emma Myles (9)
St Aloysius Primary School

SOS

As we watch the floating city sink,
We feel guilt and shame,
As we know we will not see
The Titanic sail again.
People scream and shout as they grab onto lifeboats,
And we see people jump off.
We can't believe it, we're stunned, shocked,
And meanwhile people freeze in the water,
I feel! I know! I want to do something but I can't.

We see the Titanic sinking halfway up and though,
Cups, plates, fine china are smashing inside,
Children cry for their mothers and fathers,
I know no one can save us out here,
Then the funnel falls off, *bang,* killing people.
As I look at this half sinking wall of steel,
It hurts my soul.
People are going as crazy as a troll.
Old men cling onto my lifeboat, but the rowers whack them off.

If I was one of those people getting frozen and killed,
I would be scared, frightened.
But I am not, thank goodness! I am safe
Another look round, I see the Titanic sinking badly.

Three quarters up I know their is no life,
On the Titanic, a wall of steel as I say.
10, 9, 8, 7, 6, it is too late, the Titanic has gone.
Family friends etc gone, lost.
All that's left is luggage and other things.
Why, I say, why?

The only thing I feel is guilt!

Michael Phillips (10)
St Aloysius Primary School

TITANIC SINKS

Titanic hits the iceberg,
They say it's unsinkable,
They think it's unthinkable,
It's got a lot of power,
They try and try to reverse,
But the ship has a lot of holes.

The people get in the lifeboats,
Women and children first,
Women and children from first and second class first,
They get out and go crazy.
They have officers in charge of every lifeboat,
They hit the water with a burst,
People jumping off at first,
Titanic goes down with a splash.

John Fegan (10)
St Aloysius Primary School

THE TRAGIC TITANIC

We were going along until something went wrong
But nobody knew because the captain was asleep
We got warnings that we didn't receive
Suddenly the boiler room was flooded
The captain woke up and said, 'Get the lifeboats ready'
'Quick the phone is ringing'
'What is it?'
'Sir, we are sinking'
'Lower the lifeboats, children and ladies first'
'Sir right on it.
OK everybody out! We are sinking
On top of the roof!
Ladies and children first!'

When I got into the lifeboat
I felt very sad and unhelpful
I will miss all my family and friends
This will be a big tragedy
There were only seven hundred and five people saved
And fifteen hundred people died.

Jamie McCutcheon (10)
St Aloysius Primary School

THE TITANIC

I saw the Titanic sinking,
Scared of what might happen,
And I sat there thinking,
Fifteen hundred people dead

I could get shark bite,
Afraid, frozen, guilty, helpless,
I couldn't sleep that night,
People say it's the floating city

My body had frozen,
So had my brain,
I had a blue nose,
And the Titanic had gone.

Brendan Jacobson (10)
St Aloysius Primary School

We Failed To Reach New York

Our valiant ship had failed us . . .
What were we going to do?
There was a big fuss
And a little rush
To get to the children and lifeboats too.

But now we are far away
Cold and frozen and nearly half dead
All we can do is say
Our feet feel like lead.

We're floating slowly away
Filled with guild and shame
But there's nothing we can do
Except hope.

Katy O'Donnell (10)
St Aloysius Primary School

I'M HELPLESS

Those poor people all will die
And I think it is because of me.
It is all my fault, what shall I do?
I'm helpless.
I will take guilt off all their souls
And what happens to them?
Will there be any survivors?
I'm helpless.
I wish I could get more on the lifeboat.
I got the last lifeboat and it is full.
Should I abandon or should I stay?
I'm helpless.
I need help and so do they.
I will be thinking about this
For the rest of my life.
I'm helpless.
What shall I do? Oh what shall I do?
The Titanic is breaking and people are still on it
And I am in a lifeboat, safe but cold.
I'm helpless.
Could I get someone up and they can sit beside me
And my mum and my sister.
My dad is still on the ship
And I am very very very worried about him!
Help!
I'm helpless.

Lauren Heaney (9)
St Aloysius Primary School

My Rally Car

My rally car is grey and white
At Christmas it was such a sight.
Up and down the landing floor
Until Chloe didn't want any more.
Up into first, down into second
Through the forest, round the pond,
Of this rally car I'm so fond.
Spent the day having such fun
I hope the battery's not done.

Paul McAvoy (9)
St Aloysius Primary School

I Wanna Be . . .

I wanna be a racing star
To travel in the fastest car.
To travel for Ferrari, McLaren and
Williams I don't care,
As long as they don't charge a fare.

Are you watching Eddie Irvine?
Because all the money will soon be mine.
I will be the fastest driver of all time.
You'll hear Murray Walker say
'Young Mulholland he's fine.'

Conan Mulholland (10)
St Aloysius Primary School

HOMEWORK

I hate homework it's no fun,
I'd rather eat a chocolate chip bun.
I can't wait until I leave school,
But I have to learn, not to be a fool.

I hate maths, but I like art,
After school I go on my go-kart.
That's when I have some fun,
And after that I lie out in the sun.

Neil Scullion (10)
St Aloysius Primary School

FOOTBALL CRAZY

I'm football crazy, I'm football mad
Everyone says I'm like my dad.
I support Celtic and Liverpool
And my teacher thinks I'm a fool.
I'm a striker with great speed,
To my manager I pay much heed.
Dribbling, passing and shooting,
The crowd for me are rooting.
Some day I hope to make the grade
I hope my dreams will never fade.
I'm football crazy, I'm football mad.

Patrick Agnew (10)
St Aloysius Primary School

EXCITEMENT

Excitement is school getting locked up forever.
Excitement is having a party.
Excitement is going to Coco's.
Excitement is going to the pool.
Excitement is being rich.
Excitement is having millions of ice creams.
Excitement is being young.
Excitement is being unbeatable.
Excitement is being able to fly.
Excitement is having the biggest car.

Peter Sloan (10)
St Aloysius Primary School

SPIDERS

Spiders come in all shapes and sizes.
The hair on the back of my neck rises.
Brown ones, grey ones too.
They're out to frighten you.
Hairy legs, body parts, big bulging eyes.
My sister sees them and cries.
Sticky webs hang everywhere.
Walk through them if you dare.

Alex Brookes (9)
St Aloysius Primary School

Snowy Weather

I sit and watch the snowfall,
It waits for me to come and play.
Snowball fights. Ready 1, 2, 3 . . .
'Hey watch out! Behind the tree.'
Getting hit on the face, ouch!
Now housebound because of slippery streets
Go away snow. Come out sun.

Alan Graham (9)
St Aloysius Primary School

Christmas Is . . .

Going Christmas shopping
Putting the decorations on the tree
Getting lots of cards
Getting off school, yeah!
Singing Christmas carols
Getting up early in the morning and opening presents
Going to church
Eating too much and feeling sick
Pulling crackers with your family
Watching Christmas movies.

Christina Mulholland (9)
St Aloysius Primary School

AUTUMN IS . . .

Dark, wet, cold days and nights.
Warm clothes.
Waiting a long time for Christmas.
Yellow, rust, amber carpets calling for my kicks.
Hearing the lovely firework sizzling in the sky.
Vampires, witches, devils, trick or treating.
Making shapes with sparklers.

Nadine Simpson (8)
St Aloysius Primary School

WINTER

A fresh carpet of snow waiting for my footprints.
Slippery, slippery ice that I slip on.
A warm, cosy bed on a Saturday morning.
The howling of the wind and the rattling of the rain keeping me awake.
The cheerful crackle of a warm fire keeping me warm.
Staying indoors while the snow and ice melt -
No more snowball fights, boo!
Mum's warm soup after playing outside, yum.
Wrapping up in layers as tight as a snowball.

Paul Adair (8)
St Aloysius Primary School

FRED

I look out the window, what do I see?
A fresh carpet of snow waiting for me.
I put on my clothes and run outside,
'I will build a snowman tall and wide.'
I start with the body and then the head
'I know, I will call him Fred.'
The sun rises high in the big clear sky.
Fred starts to melt, my oh my!

Shéa McGurnaghan (8)
St Aloysius Primary School

I Saw Titanic Going Down

I saw Titanic going down.
Thoughts running through my head.
Two thousand people on that boat,
One thousand people dead.

SOS won't help me now,
Nor will the 'Californian'.
I guess I'd better wrap up tight
And sleep until the morning.

How I feel sorry for the men
And children and the women,
Who are still upon that ship.
I really hope they're coming.

The violinist has stopped now,
The oboe and the flute.
The cellist and something that
Sounds very much like a lute.

I remember Titanic's launch,
In Belfast City docks.
It was sailing to Southampton,
They're unbolting the locks.

I saw Titanic going down,
She really was just great.
I just hope that next time
'Carpathia' isn't as late.

I wonder how Titanic sank,
And why it came to be,
That hundreds had died,
All before me?

Matthew O'Kane (10)
St Aloysius Primary School

Stars

Stars glow in the dark,
Showing us the way when we're lost,
Dancing in the night's sky.
Flying, prancing, leaping and jumping in the darkness,
They're scattered everywhere at night,
As if they've fallen from Heaven above,
But when morning comes they're gone.

Siobhan Phillips (10)
St Aloysius Primary School

Snow, Snow

Snow, snow,
Here and there,
Snow, snow,
Everywhere.
Put on hats,
Put on coats,
Don’t go slow,
Rush out and . . .
Shout!

Joan Caves (9)
St Aloysius Primary School

Lying In My Bed

Lying in my bed
I was lying in my bed all cosy and warm,
My little brain was thinking about Jack Frost.
I drifted off to sleep and went to Dreamland.
Jack Frost was there.

I was standing in the back garden and Jack Frost
Was coming towards me to nip me.
I ran all around the garden and I was really scared.
Then Jack caught me and nipped me so hard!

Orlagh Dillon (9)
St Aloysius Primary School

That Fateful Day

The waves came crashing against our boat,
My heart sank like the Titanic,
It brought a tear to my eye,
Death could be smelt in the air.

I cuddled my blanket,
As though I was in the water,
Those frightening faces looked up at me,
I thought I could cry.

I felt so helpless,
I hadn't even tried,
To find survivors
Among this pile.

I heard something that stabbed me in the heart,
I heard a baby cry,
Oh why, oh why?
That poor thing would die.

Suddenly I shouted,
'Look at us lying about,
There're people out there who need our help!'
The sailor cried, 'If we go back, we might die.'

I had no hope, it had all died,
Of finding that poor child.
But I heard a cry, it couldn't be, it was
That lonely child!

We found him,
I could have shouted, 'Hooray!'
I will never forget
That fateful day.

If this hadn't happened,
Would I be the same person today?

Michael Corr (10)
St Aloysius Primary School

The Loss Of The Titanic

Sailing away was so dull
from the minute we left,
knowing that may dad
was standing there
waving form the top of the ship.
I wanted them to sail
back and get him but they
wouldn't. When I was sitting there
safe in my lifeboat, I saw him go
down to the bottom of the
sea with the Titanic.

Nathan Loughead (10)
St Aloysius Primary School

BREAKFAST

I can make it myself
Cereal, nice cold milk,
Some for my baby brother,
A baby spoon, a high chair, he needs some help.
Clean up any spills.
Coke for me, Fanta for Conor,
A glass for me, a baby cup for him.
Slurp, slurp.
'Gu, gu, gu, more' he says.
'Bye, I'm away to school.'
He wants to come too and he cries.

Natalie Woods (9)
St Colman's Primary School

THE MOST IMPORTANT THING

PlayStation before school,
'Sean, breakfast time.'
I sneak upstairs to play again.
'Sean, taxi time.'
A long journey, I talk to my friends about PlayStation games.
'I have five games, I'm not lending them to you, oh all right!'
I get all the cheats.
School - we talk about games,
Home and homework.
PlayStation again.
'Sean, dinner time,'
PlayStation again.

Sean Sloan (11)
St Colman's Primary School

Let Me Stay

We go swimming every Thursday,
Let me stay.
When I get out I am so cold,
Let me stay.
When I swim about I am so hot,
Let me stay.
When we get into the bus, it's noisy
Let me out.

Mary McNulty (10)
St Colman's Primary School

Camogie

I like camogie
Hold the caman properly
Writing hand up, other hand down
Bounce the slitor, balance it while you run
Throw it and whack it, 'a goal, one nil!'
Wear your helmet for safety
'Over to me, Geraldene, pass over to me.'
'Go, go, up here and score.'
The slitor doesn't bounce, it's hard,
Don't get hit on the hands.
Tackle, noise of sticks banging, a throw in.
I run up the field, throw it up, whack it.
The people cheer, 'A goal, we win.'

Geraldene McGrillen (9)
St Colman's Primary School

After The Swimming Lesson

Quiet on the bus
Cold in the pool
Hot in the water.

We get dressed quickly
Get on the bus quickly
Get back to school quickly
Eat our dinner quickly.

Out in the playground
Still freezing, wet hair.
It soaks into my jumper and T-shirt
Then my hair dries
And I get warm again.

Gemma Goodman (10)
St Colman's Primary School

Swimming

It is slippery in the pool,
The water is cold.
We swim around to get warm.
People rush to get play time,
I hear splashes.
Under the water the voices sound like waves
When I come up the voices echo.

Jamie Toland (9)
St Colman's Primary School

REMOTE CONTROLLED CAR

Forward, forward, forward
Turn, turn, turn,
Up we hills,
Over bumps,
Over stones,
Red, red, red,
Yellow, yellow, yellow,
A machine sound.

Radio signal,
From handset to aerial,
Invisible signal,
I'm in charge,
I'm in control,
Forward, forward, forward,
Turn, turn, turn.

A hidden switch under the car,
Two big batteries,
Two more for the handset,
All set, off we go.
Forward, forward, forward,
Turn, turn, turn.

Karl O'Connor (9)
St Colman's Primary School

After The Swimming Lesson

'Get into the pool,'
'Line up properly,'
'Don't shout on the bus.'
I sit up at the back,
Cold getting out of the water,
I warm up on the bus,
I ask the driver to put on the heater,
Back to school for a hot lunch.

Christopher Monaghan (10)
St Colman's Primary School

THE MEMORY COLLECTOR

The memory collector came today,
He took all my memories away.
He said he was going to put them in a bank,
Something about him really stank!

He took away me moving house,
Now I've got the memory of a mouse.
He stole me riding on my first bike,
I've got the memory of a tyke.

How I remember riding my bike on two,
Now I feel like such a fool.
I remember my first day at school,
Then my memory's as blank as a mule.

These memories somehow are to return,
My brain is now going to burn.
I've got the brain of a bull,
My head is now so full.

Damien Nugent (10)
St Joseph's Primary School

THE MEMORY COLLECTOR

The memory collector came today
He took our favourite memories away
He had taken them from everyone he had seen
But there was one place he had not been.

He took away my mum's first day in a pool
He took away me going to school
He took away people having fun
He took away people tanning in the sun.

I said to myself, this will have to stop
Or me and my mum will go pop
I went to his house and knocked on his door
Then he pulled me in and locked me in a store.

He was planning something really bad
To get memories he hasn't had
When I got out
I could hear him shout.

My mum burst through the door
Because she couldn't take any more
His memories flew out and away
And everyone got their memories today.

Hayden Allen (10)
St Joseph's Primary School

SUNFLOWERS

The sunflowers are so bright,
I can't believe my eyes.
Like a sun shining,
So bright in the sky,
And if you take a closer look,
They could blind you with their brightness,
They relax you so much,
Especially on a sunny day.
When they bloom,
They'll be as beautiful as can be,
And if you look after them,
They will be nearly seven foot three.
Sunflowers are beautiful flowers,
Better than a daisy or a buttercup,
With their beautiful amber petals,
And dark brown centres.
They can be as beautiful
As the sun.

Clare Howie (9)
St Joseph's Primary School

My Dog

My dog is so pretty,
My dog is so fast,
She must have a bottom of a rocket,
And blast, blast, blast.

She looks so nice,
Standing there tall,
And I know one thing,
She isn't small.

But now she's gone,
Quite far away,
But we can visit her
Every single day.

Shane Brennan (8)
St Joseph's Primary School

SUNFLOWERS

Sunflowers are enjoyable and fun,
They brighten the world and enjoy everyone,
Sunflowers grow really tall,
I saw one growing up on a wall.
Sunflowers are really fun,
They shine like mini suns.
Sunflowers grow and bloom,
They will brighten up your room.
Sunflowers look like a mix of sunsets,
I would like to see a red sunflower but I haven't seen one yet.
I don't know what they look like in the sun,
Everyone can have a sunflower,
More than one.
There are other flowers, but none brighter than these,
They grow from the ground, not on bushes or trees.

Laura Hamill (8)
St Joseph's Primary School

THE MEMORY COLLECTOR

The memory collector came today,
He took all my memories and stored them away.
But he didn't care,
But I was like a bear.

He took my granda and auntie away,
But now they can't come back and play.
He took my PlayStation 2,
But now I will take revenge on you.

What a fool he was, he even took my first day at school,
And what an idea I had, I was going to push him into the pool.
He also thought he might take Hallowe'en,
But I tried to make him into a jelly bean.

We can all shout hooray,
For the rest of the day,
For he is dead,
We can all go to bed.

Jack McDonald (9)
St Joseph's Primary School

THE TOP BOARD DISASTER

It was on a Friday, I went to the pool,
And when I got in it I felt cool!
My friends told me to do the top!
Guess what? I did a belly flop!

I got out of the cool pool
And my shorts were baggy.
So I walked a little bit to the first board
I looked at my shorts and they went saggy!

Daniel Burns (10)
St Joseph's Primary School

THE MEMORY COLLECTOR

The memory collector came today,
He took my favourite memories away.
Then he put them all in a sack,
And said, 'I need more - I will be back!'

Into the sack went my first birthday,
And in went my first holiday.
He took away my first day at school,
And my first Christmas - it was cool!

He took my first word, he took my first bike,
He took all the things I used to like.
Away went the first time a friend came to stay,
Away went my favourite day.

When the memory collector went away,
I tried to think what had happened today.
I didn't remember - he'd taken that too,
So I hope he doesn't come to you!

Ellen Watters (9)
St Joseph's Primary School

THE MEMORY COLLECTOR

The memory collector came today,
He took all my memories away.
As he threw his sack over his back,
He cried 'Ha, ha, ha, they are all in my sack.'

First, he took away my memory of Christmas,
Then the snow we had, next the first time I went to mass,
Then he took the memory of my granda dying,
I can't remember if I was crying.

How could he take my memory of the seaside?
The buckets, spades, and in school who do I sit beside?
He took away my first time flying,
And the memory of my great aunt dying.

I saw the memory collector again today,
The person who took my memories away,
Then I noticed my memories were out of his sack
I knew I would get them back.

Laura Benson (10)
St Joseph's Primary School

Ice Cream

I like ice cream
When it's hot
It tastes good
With sprinkles on top

The best thing about it
Is that it cools you down
My favourite flavour is
Raspberry with a little
Cherry on top.

Kathleen McMahon (10)
St Joseph's Primary School

My Pets

My dog is cool,
Her name is Tip,
She really would like a swim in the pool,
She does make a tip of the house,
Tip is the coolest and the best dog in the world!

My gerbil is really fantastic,
Her name is Noodles,
Because her tail looks like one,
She is quick and small,
She might break the law one day by stealing food,
Noodles is fantastic!

My pets are the coolest pets I've ever had.

Ana Clarke (10)
St Joseph's Primary School

DOORBELLS

You walk to the door
You can't get in
You look for a knocker
You just can't win.

Then you see the bell
Shiny and clean
You don't know what sound
It will make you wait
For the chime it
Is fine. No one is
In that's all right
You will come
Again!

Sean Comiskey (11)
St Joseph's Primary School

Stock Cars

Have you ever been in a race
especially against time?
My friend tells me it can hurt your spine.
When the seat belt hits you
it's like your back has broken,
but even more when the door jams you in.

Stephen McGrath (11)
St Joseph's Primary School

CARS

Lots of cars are really fast,
when they go they'll make you laugh.
There are lots of cars that go in the dust,
but then again some have rust.
Cars are fast, cars are slow.
I know that when I see them go.

Ciaran Connolly (11)
St Joseph's Primary School

Hot Poker

There is a very hot poker
that sits in the fire
gleaming red
which is very warm.

The colour is black
which is very shiny
and it's like a fire
'cause of the colour
on the end of a poker.

Martin Frazer (11)
St Joseph's Primary School

THE MEMORY COLLECTOR

One day a man came to town
He collected my memory, I thought I lost my crown
He scooped it up in a jar and said 'Thank you'
But then I said 'You are who?'

Out of mind and into the jar
Came the first time I was in the car
Then came the picture of me wearing a diaper
Then the rifle that was a sniper.

Next came my birthdays
And all the Christmas days
Then the first day at school
And the first time I supported Liverpool

And the day I got Chaz, the hamster
And the day my mum taught me to stir
Next came the day I saw Harry Potter
And the day my mum gave up the lottery.

The day I got my bike
And the day I got the Game Boy advance
Plus the day I went to Letterkenny
And the first day I ate Denny's ham.

So I knocked him to the ground.
He gave me a pound.
Then I got my memory back
I said 'Thank you' and gave him a smack.

Daniel Wilson (9)
St Joseph's Primary School

THE MEMORY COLLECTOR

The memory collector came today,
He stole my favourite memories away,
I cried 'Come back with your enormous sack!
Give me my favourite memories back!'

He took away my youngest sister,
Left me nothing but her blister,
Then he took my very first word,
And left me nothing that had occurred.

He took away my first day at school,
(I thought that was rather cool),
I forgot my mummy telling me she was pregnant,
Away went the first time I saw my best aunt.

He even took my very first step,
Away went the first time I play zep.
He took away the first time I rode on two wheels,
And the time I had my three-course meals.

With no memories, life was a bore,
The memories we had, are now no more,
So open up your big sack,
And give me all of them back.

Caoimhe Dawson (10)
St Joseph's Primary School

THE SWIMMING DISASTER

One day I was walking into the pool,
I was really trying to act quite cool,
But then I tripped,
I got up again, but then I *slipped.*

Then my friends came, they were going to do the dive,
But I thought to myself, will I come out dead or alive?
Then I saw the lifeguard and I thought if I drown, will he save me?
I will just fly off the board like a bumblebee.

So I jumped off the top board
And I was praying to the Lord
I heard my knuckles go pop
And then I did a really big bellyflop.

When I got out, my friends were laughing at me
I really wasn't like a bumblebee
I will never forget that day
Never, never again, no way!

Gemma Carey (10)
St Joseph's Primary School

Going To The Swimming Pool

I went to the swimming pool
When I got out I was such a fool,
I was still wearing my pants
So I hid behind the plants!

Jamie Gaffey (9)
St Joseph's Primary School

My Dog Hamish

My dog Hamish likes to play,
He always does what I say,
Like 'Sit,' 'Leave,' 'Lie down!'
But when I'm asleep, he won't make a sound.

Hamish is my best friend in the whole wide world
When he sleeps, he's always curled,
Hamish is very cute and sweet,
And he really likes to eat meat.

Hamish would never ever bite,
But if a stranger came in, he just might,
Hamish and I have a good friendship,
And when he runs he has a wobbly lip.

I'd sit and watch Hamish for hours and hours,
Hamish doesn't like flowers,
Hamish and I are special friends,
And so our friendship will never end.

Sinead Crilley (11)
St Joseph's Primary School

FISH

Fish, fish, what are fish?
Wonderful, slippery, slimy fish,
They swim around all day long
If you listen carefully you might hear a song,
That is a bird coming along to eat the fish,
The slippery fish you might see on your dish,
But please don't eat that poor wee fish.

Enya Brennan (11)
St Joseph's Primary School

THE MEMORY COLLECTOR

The memory collector came today
He took all my memories far away
I sat and sighed and moaned in gloom
Were all my memories about to meet their doom?

Some were boring, some were fun
Some were of me in the sun
All these he took, with not one to spare
Chase after him . . . I didn't dare

He took away memories of me as a tyke
He took away memories of my first bike
I forget what age I was when I started school
Or when I learnt to swim in a swimming pool.

He took away memories of me in Donegal
Or when I first kicked a ball
Or when I went to Tyrella Beach
Or when I disliked my first taste of peach.

Then he came back with a huge bulging head
'Take them back,' he said, 'they're as heavy as lead.'
I jumped up and shouted with lots of glee
Now all my memories are back with me.

Michael Kelly (9)
St Joseph's Primary School

THE MEMORY COLLECTOR

The memory man came today
And stole all my wonderful memories away
He put all my memories in his sack
Don't do that, give me my memories back.

He took my first pony
And my thoughtful friend Tony
Next he took my memory when I first walked
And when I first talked.

He took my lovely niece away
Please bring her back, but please go away
Next he took away Donegal
He took all my friends away
And he took my favourite ball away.

Orla McCartan (10)
St Joseph's Primary School

WINTER

A sheet of snow everywhere
Nothing else in sight,
Everyone has on gloves
They don't want a chill bite.

Children are outside
Playing with the snow,
Making lots of snowballs
All ready for them to throw.

Then all the children sit by the fire
Warming each and every toe,
They're inside all cosy and warm
Out of the cold, cold snow.

Barbara Fleming (11)
St Joseph's Primary School

The Memory Collector

The memory collector came today,
He took my memories all away.
He took all the good things that were in my mind,
Now I didn't have any memories to find.

First he took my auntie away,
Then he took my bike away, so I had nothing to play,
He took my granda who was super cool,
But then he took my first day in school.

Then he took my first Christmas ever,
He took my birthday. Never!
But then he took my holiday which was cool,
And then he took my favourite pool.

Life has been dull and thinking has been grey,
Whenever he took my memories away.
Then I saw them in his sack,
I guessed I would get them back.

Rachel Jennings (10)
St Joseph's Primary School

The Memory Collector

The memory collector came today
He took all my memories away,
He managed to put them in his sack,
Which was carried upon his back.

He carried away my first day of school,
And my memories beside the pool,
Next was my cousin Niamh,
And the time when I started to teeth.

Followed by my holiday in Salou,
And all my fond memories of you,
Then went Christmas and many more,
Also when my trouser leg tore.

When the memory collector came back,
All my memories fell out of his sack,
Now my memories are in my head,
The next time he comes back I will dread.

Aíne Molloy (10)
St Joseph's Primary School

THE SUNFLOWERS

I had some sunflowers,
That grew very tall,
I couldn't see a thing at all,
They grew and grew very big,
All I could see
Were some bright, burning flowers,
The sunflowers were amber,
And some were green,
And if you looked at them,
They made you have a warm feeling.
They bloom in summer,
They are very bright,
They look like real bright suns,
You can always see them,
You would never miss them,
Even in the night, that shows they're very bright.
They turn towards the sun.

Emma Ross (8)
St Joseph's Primary School

The Mummy's Tomb

There's treasure in the pyramid
Hidden down below,
Down beneath the golden sand
Where only brave folk go.

Down and down the passageway
Watching where you tread,
Trying not to make a sound
Or wake up all the dead.

'Hooray!' cried all the spooky ghosts,
'You're really not a dummy.'
'Take the treasure, it's all yours,
You've won it!' cried the mummy.

Claire Soult (9)
St Joseph's Primary School

The Crocodile In The Nile

On the faraway island of Zalamondeach,
A sly, sneaky crocodile lay on the beach,
He sat for a while, then jumped in the Nile,
The fish had to dash because of the splash.

The crocodile had ruined his dinner,
And got so much thinner.

Ben McMullan (9)
St Joseph's Primary School

The Sunflower

Every day I go out and see
My sunflower blooming brightly.
I water it very, very carefully,
Ever since the seed was in the ground,
I adored it, my very own sunflower.

The beautiful burnt orange,
It's like I'm walking into
A beautiful, bright imaginary
Room of my very own.

It is like I am on a beach,
Watching the sunset.
My sunflower is like a mini sun,
It makes me feel warm on cold days.

Amy Stinton (9)
St Joseph's Primary School

THE MEMORY COLLECTOR

The memory collector came today,
He took all my memories away,
He took them in a sack,
I'm sure he'll be back,

He took all my memories away,
I hated him that day,
He stole my memories when I was in school,
But I didn't look very cool,

He stole my first bed,
With a pencil lead,
I hated him that much,
I put him on a crutch,

He stole my pet,
Which I wouldn't let,
So I went to the sack,
And pulled my pet back,

Since he took my memory away,
I don't think he came back that day,
He ran away with his heavy sack,
Oh, I'm sure he won't be back.

Jordan Taggart (10)
St Joseph's Primary School

The Memory Collector

The memory collector came today,
And stole all my fantastic memories away.
He said 'I've got them in my sack,
And some day I'll bring them back.'

He took my memory of Granda Keown,
And he even took my classic phone.
Then he took my first word,
And my memory of a bird.

Then he took my very first crib
Oh no, not my bib!
He took my memory of falling into a bath,
And my memory of seeing my first café.

In went my bike,
Which I really liked.
He stole my cat,
Which was a bit fat.

One day the memory collector came back,
With his huge, big sack.
He opened up his huge, great sack,
And I had all my memories back.

Emma Maguire (10)
St Joseph's Primary School

The Memory Collector

The memory collector came today
He took all my memories away
He took away his filled sack
Which I thought he was bringing back

He took away my holiday
Where I used to lie on the bay
He took away my first day of school
Which I thought was really cool

He also took my new car
Which I always took far
He took away my shark balloon
From where I played with it in the pool

He took away my mask
Where someone put me on a task
He also took my Game Boy
With which I have a lot of joy.

Since he took my memory away
He would never come back that day
After that he came back another day
He did not get anything away.

Grant Humphreys (10)
St Joseph's Primary School

THE MEMORY COLLECTOR

The memory collector came today,
And took all my precious memories away.
'Don't worry,' said Mum, 'you know he's bad,
But without our memories, we'll all be so sad.'

He took away my first day of school,
Even my first lesson in the swimming pool,
How could you take my nana Lily?
And he also took me being silly.

No, you don't, not me naming my first teddy,
Or the time I first ate spaghetti.
You've guessed it, he took my first tooth,
And when I was sick at the Pizza Hut booth.

I won't let you take my kitten,
Or when I just tried knitting.
Don't you dare take me moving house,
Even when I got a mouse.

The memory collector came today,
But he didn't take any more memories away,
Just then he opened his sack,
And before we knew it, we had our memories back!

Amy Kerr (10)
St Joseph's Primary School

THE BUNGEE-JUMPING MESS-UP

This is a story that is head-hurting
And it will make you go turning
I went to a bridge to bungee-jump off
If you look down at it, it makes you go soft

I thought I was a woman too scared
Even though I was prepared
I went to jump off and off I did go
As fast as I could go (not very slow)

Just then I heard a great *snap!*
I was flying so high, even higher than a cat!
I went diving into a big river
It was so deep I couldn't even shiver

When I woke up I looked around
Everything I saw was completely round
Just then I found myself in hospital,
But it looked more like a shabby hostel

To this day I'm still quaking
You could almost think I'm shaking
This is my sorrowful story
Hope you cried and you're not looking for more!

Conor Drayne (10)
St Joseph's Primary School

TELEVISION

Television, television
You are great.
Oh how I love to watch you
With all those great programmes.

Television, television
You sit in my living room
All alone and turned off.
Oh tele, oh tele, I think you are great.
Come with me and you
Won't be lonely.

Finnian McKeown (11)
St Joseph's Primary School

SUMMER

Summer is good and lots of fun
It is hot and sunny and really cool
Children out in the street
Clatter, patter of the feet.
Splash, splash, children playing in paddling pools
Bash, crash, bash, kids fighting
Over the last lollipop because it is so hot.

Wish, woe, went the waves of the sea.
To me this is the best to be.
People queuing for miles on end for a lollipop
Like it's the latest trend.

Summer watches over you,
Leaving the winter behind
School is gone for so long.
Oh what fun it will be sun, sand and sea.

Jeanette Johnson (11)
St Joseph's Primary School

THE TORTOISE

I am a little tortoise wandering up the stairs
Everybody leaves me and nobody cares.
Trying to get up those steep, steep stairs
How can I because nobody cares.
The rabbit and the hare just bounce up those stairs,
But I'm on my own because nobody cares.
How can I get up those steep, steep stairs?
But if I do, somebody might care.

Ciara Heaney (10)
St Joseph's Primary School

WINTER

Winter, winter, as cold as ice.
Winter, winter, as frozen as snow.
Winter, winter, how wet can it get?
Winter, winter, as frozen as me.
Winter, winter, as cold as a bee.
Winter, winter, as white as can be.
Winter, winter, not as hot as me.
Winter, winter, as we can see.
Winter, winter, a very cold day.
Winter, winter, with a wet, windy day.
Winter, winter, not with a wet day.
Winter, winter, as dark as the night's sky.
Winter, winter, as wet as a water tap.

Richard McConnel (10)
Old Warren Primary School

WINTER

Winter, winter, black as night,
Leaves yellow, as the sun,
Winter, cold as ice,
Snow, cold as water,
Trees, bare as me,
I love winter, don't go away,
Stay, stay with me,
Snow gives me the shivers,
Jack Frost gives me the cold,
I want you to stay,
I want you to stay,
Don't go away,
Don't go away,
Just come and stay,
Winter, winter, black as night,
I like you winter,
Please come and stay,
I like you winter, don't go away.

Jemma-Louise McDonagh (10)
Old Warren Primary School

Winter

Winter, winter, as cold as cold water.
Winter, winter, as dark as a black cat.
Winter, winter, as boring as a drawing.
Winter, winter, as white as rice.
Winter, winter, as long as summer.
Winter, winter, snow as white as paper.

Scott Brooks (10)
Old Warren Primary School